# Families and their Faiths

# Hinduism in Bali

Written by Frances Hawker and Putu Resi
Photography by Bruce Campbell

Cherrytree Books

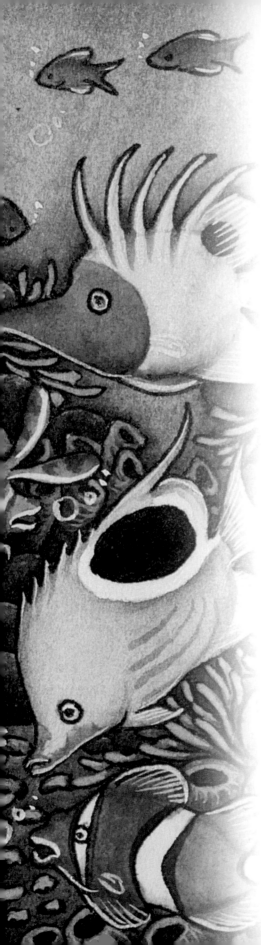

A Cherrytree Book

Published in 2008 by
Cherrytree Books, part of
Evans Publishing Group
2a Portman Mansions
Chiltern Street
London W1U 6NR

British Library Cataloguing in Publication Data
Hawker, Frances
   Hinduism in Bali. - (Families and their faiths)
   1. Hinduism - Indonesia - Bali - Juvenile literature
   2. Dance - Religious aspects - Hinduism - Juvenile
   literature 3. Bali (Indonesia) - Religious life and customs
   - Juvenile literature
   I. Title II. Campbell, Bruce
   294.5'095986

ISBN 9781842345054

Editor: Su Swallow
Designer: Robert Walster, Big Blu Design
Printed in Dubai by Oriental Press

Frances Hawker and Bruce Campbell have travelled all round the world, beginning when they made their way overland from Europe to Australia thirty-five years ago. They have previously published ten children's books together.

Putu Resi acted as coordinator, translator and adviser on the cultural aspects of the book. She is the keeper of a temple at Sindhu beach in Sanur, Bali, and is greatly involved with dance performances.

Artwork by Ketut Suardana

Half of the royalties from the sales of this series will go to the local communities featured in the books.

VISIT OUR WEBSITE
Evans
www.evansbooks.co.uk

For more information about the authors and about the people and places featured in this book, please go to our website www.evansbooks.co.uk

# Contents

This is a story about my granddaughter, Yoni. I have ten grandchildren. Yoni is the youngest. She is seven years old. We live on the small island of Bali, in Indonesia.

Here we are dressed up for a special ceremony at the temple.

I run a small café on the beach. It is called a *warung*. People come to my café while the children play and swim in the sea.

Yoni likes to watch me cook. The people of Bali like hot, spicy food. I grind the spices and hot chillies with a stone.

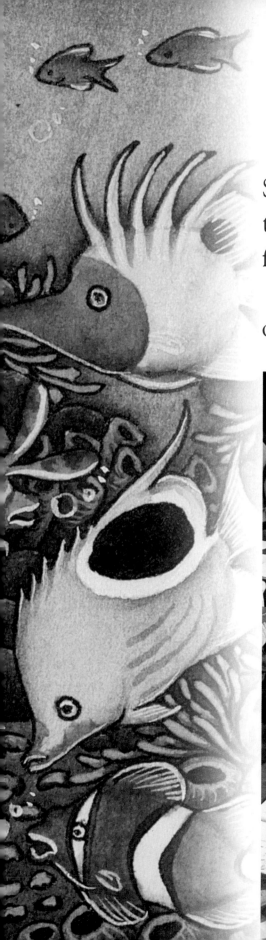

Yoni wakes early each morning to go to school. School starts at half past seven, and finishes at ten o'clock. Yoni is in class one, and there are forty children in her class.

Every morning the children pray to the goddess of learning, Saraswati, to help them at school.

In the afternoons Yoni likes to swim with her
friends. There is a calm lagoon in front of our
house. Yoni's uncle, Made, likes to fish with his
net. He catches small fish in the shallow water
for us to eat for dinner.

Yoni's great-grandfather makes musical instruments for the gamelan orchestra. He uses spells and chants to give them a magical sound.

Yoni wants to learn to play.

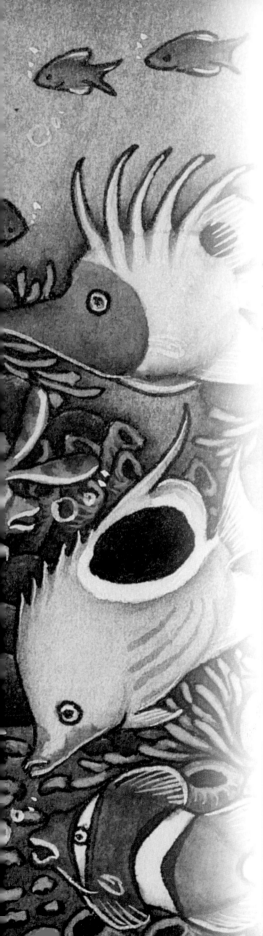

Like most Balinese we are Hindus.

Dancing is very important to our faith. Yoni and her friends have dance lessons. Before their lessons they go to the temple to thank the gods for the gift of dancing.

I help Yoni to make offerings for the gods. We fold coconut leaves into boxes and fill them with flowers. There are red petals for Brahma, white petals for Shiva and green leaves for Wisnu.

We light incense sticks so the smoke carries our prayers and gifts up to the gods.

We give small offerings several times each day. Women put them in the family temples and around the house. Bus drivers put them at crossroads, where spirits meet. Musicians place them on their instruments.

We make larger offerings for ceremonies. We take piles of rice cakes and fruit to the temple. A priest blesses them.

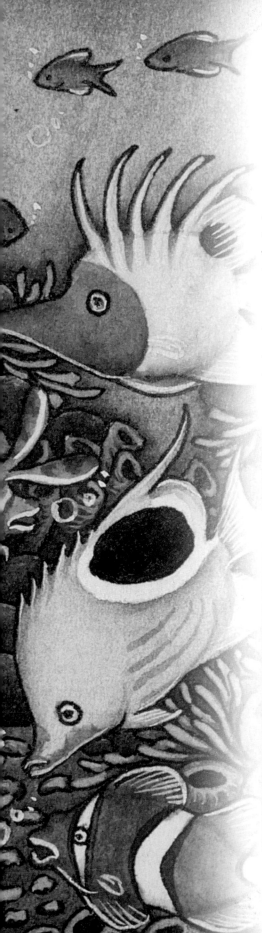

Dancing is a gift from the gods to our family.
I used to be a dancer, and so did Yoni's mother.
Now she teaches the children of the village.

Children learn to dance with their body, arms,
legs, head and even their eyes.

The girls giggle as they get ready to dance at my *warung.*

Tourists and local people come to enjoy the dance and the music.

Many of our dances tell stories. Some of the stories come from a famous Hindu story called the *Ramayana.*

In this dance Yoni shakes the trees and collects the most perfect flowers that fall to the ground. She makes these into a beautiful headdress for a princess.

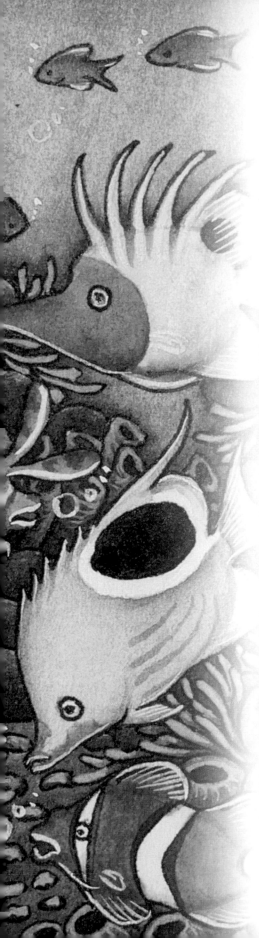

Here Yoni is a bird trying to protect the queen. The dance is very long. Yoni has to remember every flick of the eyes, every twist of the fingers and every turn of the toes.

Yoni practises for a special ceremony at the temple. She practises the dance over and over for weeks. She will not stop until it is perfect.

On the day of the ceremony Yoni wakes up early. She is very excited. Yoni's mother dresses her to look beautiful as she dances for the gods. She wraps her in eight metres of gold printed material. Then she winds a yellow cloth around her waist. Finally she places a crown with gold, jewels and flowers on her head.

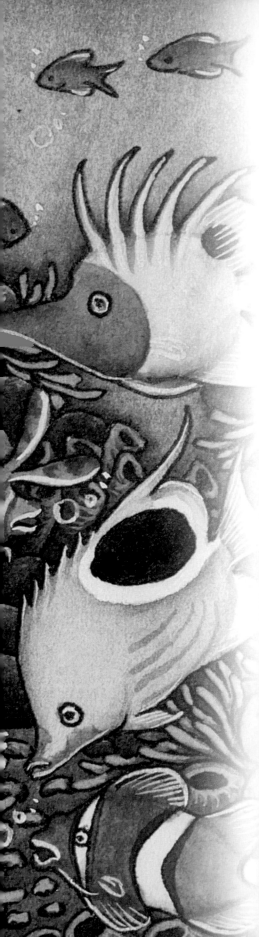

We all dress up for the ceremony. It is to bless and purify the temple. We know that our gods and the spirits of our ancestors will come for the celebrations and prayers. Everything must be perfect.

Yoni is worried about the dance. What if she forgets something?

Yoni watches as a priest blesses the other little
dancers. Their costumes glisten in the sunlight.

They dance to welcome the visiting spirits. The
temple has no roof so we are linked to the gods
above. We can hear the priests chanting.

Suddenly there is a loud clanging from the gamelan orchestra. A boy dancer leaps on to the floor. He looks fierce in his ancient warrior's costume. On his back he wears a dagger that has magical powers. He is the guardian of the visiting spirits. He spins and stamps and charges. The music plays louder and louder, faster and faster, until the warrior's dance suddenly ends.

24

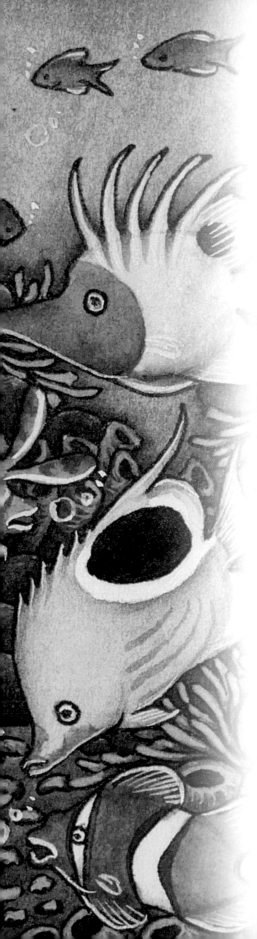

The dance is just too scary for little Wayan.
She starts to cry, and Made comforts her.

The time has come for Yoni to dance. I pray to the gods that she will dance beautifully. The men in the gamelan orchestra can sense the power of the dance. They play better than ever.

There is a hush in the crowd. Everyone can feel the magic. Yoni has been blessed with *taksu*. The spirit of the dance has entered into her and is dancing with her.

The gods are happy with our little dancer.

And so are we.

# Notes for Parents and Teachers

For more information about the authors and the people and places featured in this book, please go to our website: www.evansbooks.co.uk

Hinduism began in India at least 5000 years ago. It is the world's oldest religion, and has approximately a billion followers, mainly in India and Nepal. Hindus believe that everything comes from an eternal spirit called Brahman, the source of all life. Hindus worship many gods and goddesses. Three of the most important are Brahma, Wisnu and Shiva.

Balinese Hinduism is a fusion of different traditions. Balinese culture is rich and the people follow the traditions passed down from their ancestors. Bali is full of things you cannot see: gods, goddesses, good spirits, demons, bad spirits, prayers, spells and magic.

Hindus believe in *samsara*. They believe that this life is just one of many that they experience. If someone leads a good life, their next one will be better. If they live a bad life, their next one will be worse.

Hindus believe that they are reincarnated. When they die they are born again in a new body to lead another life. If someone finally leads a perfect life then they may get off the wheel of reincarnation and achieve a perfect state called *moksa*.

### Page 6

Each child in Yoni's school must help clean the school when they arrive. They have their own broom and must help sweep the room and the outside area, wipe down the desks and, once a week, clean the windows.

Yoni's lessons finish at ten o'clock in the morning, and at eleven o'clock another year one class arrives and uses the same room.

### Pages 8 and 9

Usually only boys and men play in gamelan orchestras. The bronze keys of the

30

instruments make a wonderful, clear sound when they are hit with a wooden hammer.

There is no written music for these instruments. Small boys sit on their fathers' laps and learn by listening and watching over and over at ceremonies and practices.

### Pages 11, 12 and 13

Offerings are given to spirits and ancestors, as well as gods. They are treated with great respect (see notes to page 22). Balinese give offerings not only to good spirits, but to bad ones too, to keep them happy.

Offerings need to be beautiful and are made from things the gods have given to people in nature, such as flowers, fruit, and leaves. These are given back to the gods as thanks. Small offerings include whole flowers or petals, cut fruit and chopped pandanus leaves.

Large offerings that are taken to the temple are blessed by a priest, and then carried home on women's heads and eaten. They can include flowers, fruit, rice cakes, and decorations made from woven palm fronds. Sometimes people can place whole roast piglets on the offerings.

### Pages 14 and 15

Dancing really does run in Yoni's family. Her great-grandfather was a dancer who danced at temple festivals. Her grandmother was a *janger* dancer and danced and sang in a group of five girls and five boys. Although Yoni is only seven years old she is already a talented dancer. She has won many dance competitions that are run between different villages. She has also won a prize for the best little dancer in Bali on Balinese television.

### Pages 16 and 17

The *Ramayana* is an epic poem, which tells the story of Rama and his wife, Sita. It has 24,000 verses, and is thought to have been composed some 5000 years ago. The poem forms part of the Hindu scriptures.

### Page 22

During this ceremony gods and ancestors visit their worshippers and relatives. Temples in Bali are in simple open courtyards where people can communicate directly with their gods.

### Page 23

These dancers are called *rejang dewa* dancers. They welcome and entertain the visiting spirits. This is a sacred dance and can only be danced at religious ceremonies.

# Glossary

| | |
|---|---|
| Ancestor | A relative who died a long time ago |
| Gamelan | A group of musical instruments from Indonesia |
| Headdress | Decorated covering for the head |
| Incense | Something that is burned to make a pleasant smell |
| Lagoon | A calm area of sea, protected by a reef |
| Offering | A gift given to the gods to thank them or ask for help |
| Purify | To clean something thoroughly |
| Ramayana | A long poem telling the story of Rama and Sita. It is part of the Hindu scriptures |
| Taksu | A performance that is guided by the gods |
| Tradition | An old custom or belief |
| Warung | The Indonesian name for a café |

# Index